SUPERIOR FLIES

Books by Leonard M. Wright, Jr.

Fishing the Dry Fly as a Living Insect

Trout Heresies

Where the Fish Are

The Ways of Trout

First Cast

The Masters on the Nymph (ed., with J. M. Migel)

Superior Flies

SUPERIOR FLIES

Leonard M. Wright, Jr.

Illustrations by John Robert White

Nick Lyons Books

LYONS & BURFORD, PUBLISHERS

THE CORTLAND LIBRARY

This fine book is one of a continuing series, sponsored by Cortland Line Company, Inc., Cortland, New York, designed for all fly fishermen—from beginning to advanced sportsmen. The series currently includes *Fly Rodding for Bass* by Charles F. Waterman, *Superior Flies* by Leonard M. Wright, Jr., *Practical Salt Water Fly Fishing* by Mark Sosin, and *Wade a Little Deeper, Dear: A Woman's Guide to Fly Fishing* by Gwen Cooper and Evelyn Haas.

© 1989 by Leonard M. Wright, Jr.
Illustrations © 1989 by John Robert White

Printed in the United States of America

10   9   8   7   6   5   4   3   2

Library of Congress Cataloging-in-Publication Data

Wright, Leonard M.
    Superior flies/Leonard M. Wright, Jr.; illustrations by John Robert White.
        p.   cm.—(The Cortland library)
    Includes bibliographical references.
    ISBN 1-55821-042-3: $8.95
    1. Flies, Artificial. I. Title. II. Series.
SH451.W753   1989
688.7'912—dc20

89-37570
CIP

Contents

Introduction

There are dozens—probably hundreds—of books on the market that tell you how to *tie* flies. But I've never seen even one that tells you how to *buy* them.

This, I feel, is a glaring omission. Most fly fishers aren't fly tyers. The majority of us have to buy, borrow, or steal the flies we fish with—and we need guidance. Even beginning or intermediate tyers would benefit from a book that pointed out the subtle qualities that make for excellence in individual flies.

I have run across only two books that even touch on this subject: Datus Proper's *What the Trout Said* and C. F. Walker's *Fly-Tying as an Art*. While both deal with trout flies only and dry flies mostly, I can't recommend them too highly. They'll start you looking at, and critiquing, all your flies in a far more perceptive manner.

There is probably no such thing as a perfect fly, but some artificials are obviously far superior to others. Proportions may be the thing to look for in some types of ties. Quality of materials may be crucial in others. Often both are essential to excellence. But how do you judge these elements? What yardsticks can you use?

And, since there are literally thousands of listed patterns on record, which ones should you buy? What makes up a good, basic selection for trout? For bass? For salt water? For the southern flats? And how many duplicates should you carry for a day's fishing?

Such questions don't have pat answers. In most cases, I'll pass on to you the recommendations of the most skillful anglers I know—even though these are rarely unanimous. There are bound to be varying judgments on, say, the relative importance of color, design, size, or action to a fly's overall effectiveness. But I'll give you the majority opinions.

In a few instances, I'll state strong—but purely personal—preferences. When I do, I'll explain the reasons for my prejudices and, if you're not persuaded, feel free to ignore them.

The aim of this book, then, is simple and straightforward: to focus your attention on the flies you choose and use. If it succeeds in this, even half way, it will have made you, in a very short time, into a far more effective fly fisher.

LEONARD M. WRIGHT, JR.
New York City
December 1988

SUPERIOR FLIES

The Importance of Being Excellent

The first and great commandment in fly fishing is so simple and self-evident that it is often forgotten. *The only part of your tackle that any fish should ever see is your fly.*

Fly fishers talk a lot about the actions of the latest graphite fly rods and the smoother drags on new reels, but give little lip-service to the finer points of artificial flies. I can't understand this. Fish aren't attracted or deceived by rods and reels. But they most certainly are by flies.

I am acquainted with several wealthy, self-indulgent anglers who own staggering inventories of expensive rods and reels. And, yes, they own box after box of flies, too. Yet these are filled with shop-tied flies that are, at best, mediocre.

I haven't the heart to point out to them that for the price of one of their vintage bamboos, they could buy a lifetime supply of superior flies, custom-tied out of the choicest materials by a world-class professional. It seems they'd rather impress their peer-group than the fish.

Obviously, they've bought their flies from some prestigious tackle company. But ordering a dozen size #10 dry March Browns from a catalog is like ordering "a car" from General Motors. You'd have no idea which make, model, color, and optional extras they'd send you.

Similarly, your March Browns could be quite a surprise. Would they be tied sparsely or bushily? Would they have stiff or soft hackles? Would the bodies be brown or yellowish? I don't care what the color plate in the catalog may show, it gives you little idea of what you'll probably receive. Unless you're familiar with an individual fly tyer's style and standards for materials, buying flies sight-unseen is usually a waste of money.

Of course, the ideal situation is to be an expert fly tyer yourself, with a vast array of the finest furs and feathers at your fingertips. Next best is to be a personal friend of a first-rate amateur or professional who will custom-tie patterns to your exact specifications. Unfortunately, very few fly fishers fall into either of these two privileged categories.

Which Tyer?

The first step the average angler should take is to try to locate the tyer or shopkeeper in his area who offers the best-tied flies and uses the choicest materials. Question the skillful fly fishermen you know or meet—especially those who tie their own. You'll soon narrow the field down to one or two choices, but, even then, you're only halfway home.

Cream of His Crop

Let's say you now enter your chosen shop to buy several dry Light Cahills in size #14. There are liable to be dozens in the compartment so labelled. But all flies—even those tied by the same person—are not created equal. You'll want to walk out with the three very best of the bunch. What should you look for—and look *out* for?

Which Patterns? How Many?

Then there's the dilemma of how many patterns you should own and in which sizes. Another question is how many duplicates you should carry for a day's fishing. Dry flies can get soggy or chewed up and need changing. Any type of fly can get damaged or lost to a fish, snag, or tree. Unless you're willing to stagger around with a huge inventory in your vest, you'll have to make some shrewd— often agonizing—decisions.

Basic Colors

On the brighter side, most (though not all) insect, bait-minnow, and crustacean species fall into a relatively few color schemes or color combinations. This allows you to put together a modest working inventory that should cover the vast majority of situations. There are, however, special, atypical flies you'd be lost without at certain times and places. The early-summer hatches of huge salmon flies (a species of stone fly) in the Rockies is a good example. Another is the spawning swarm of red worms during a few nights a year on the Florida tarpon flats. I can't, in this space, point out all the regional "specials." You'll just have to pry these secrets out of the locals when you're in alien territory. But it's essential that you learn them.

Hooks

Though this is a book about flies, not hardware, I can't neglect hooks completely because these essential irons are the only thing all flies have in common. Every fly starts out in life as a naked hook. The problem is that with already-tied flies, the decision as to which make, model, size, and weight of hook to use has already been made for you by the fly tyer.

Shopkeepers and professional tyers are accustomed to a lot of browsing and fondling of their products and have learned to tolerate this. But if you start testing the hooks on their flies and bending some out of shape, you'll probably be evicted.

Fortunately, the vast majority of flies are tied on hooks that are quite satisfactory. The heavy-wire models used for most wet flies, nymphs, streamers, and salt-water flies usually possess adequate hooking qualities and are strong enough to handle most of the fish you'll tie into.

Dry flies are another matter. Makers of light-wire hooks have to decide how much weight or how much strength can be sacrificed. Then there's the matter of temper. If the steel is too soft, the hook will bend out easily and stay that way. If the hook is too hard, the hook-bend will be brittle and likely to snap under pressure. Those with ideal temper yield a bit under pressure then spring back to their original shape.

But it's the tyer's job, not yours, to test and select. It is comforting to know that most top-notch tyers use first-rate hooks.

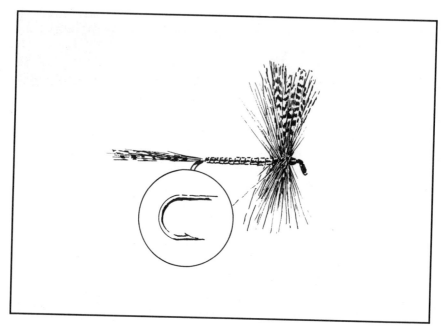

Fig. 1 Dry fly on perfect bend hook—detail

I personally prefer round-bend hooks with short points and small barbs for my floaters (see Figure 1). The old Allcock Model Perfects were aptly named, but they're no longer available. I have found most light-wire Partridges and Tiemcos excellent and there are probably others just as good. Heavy-wire Mustads are usually good, but some of their lighter models are soft-tempered and offer a stingy hook gape in the smaller sizes. You'll have to ask the proprietor what make and weight of hook his dries are tied on and make your own decisions.

Lastly, once you have assembled your ideal collection of best-of-litter flies (if, indeed, this process ever ends) there are ways to improve some of them. And all will lead longer, more useful lives if you follow certain precautions and procedures. These last two points are not trivial, for fish vote with their mouths and they elect superior flies year after year.

The Sincerest Flattery
Some Basics of Imitation

Over a hundred years ago, the legendary George Selwyn Marryat was asked by a skunked angler what pattern he was using to take trout after trout out of the Itchen.

His reported reply: "It's not the fly, it's the driver." (To appreciate the wit of the remark, it helps to know that a sporty, two-person, horse-drawn carriage was commonly called a "fly" back in those days.)

British fly fishers like to retell the anecdote, but the story never rang true to me—not so much because the remark lacks the self-effacing tone you'd expect of a Victorian gentleman but because it makes Marryat appear to believe that the presentation of a fly was all-important whereas we know that he, like his more famous disciple, Frederic M. Halford, was a devout "Exact Imitationist."

These men dyed all sorts of materials in their attempts to reproduce the precise colors of the common aquatic insects. They carried this so far that they came up with separate imitations for the subtly different shades of the males and females of each species.

If you examine examples of Halford's dry flies (he abhorred wets) you will notice that they all have a dense collar of hackle. He obviously believed that a dry fly should float as high off the water as possible and made no attempt to limit his artificials to the six legs that are characteristic of all insects. So I feel it would be more accurate to re-label the Marryat-Halford school "Exact Colorist."

The lesson here is that every artificial fly is a compromise of some sort. Some aspect of realism has to be sacrificed to enhance another. The presence of the hook itself and the inherent limitations in materials make this so.

For example, many of those Hornberg patterns that are so popular in northern New England present an excellent imitation of the scale-pattern of small baitfish by using barred grey mallard feathers for wings. But, to attain this, the desirable translucent quality of polar bear hair is lost. Every fly pattern is a trade-off. Each tyer makes a conscious (or unconscious) decision as to which aspect of a fly is most important to the fish.

This win-one, lose-one situation is, perhaps, most pronounced in dry-fly styles. Generally, tyers in limestone or spring creek areas emphasize precise body color and wing silhouette at the expense of flotation. Fish in glassy-surfaced streams eyeball a fly for several seconds before tilting up and taking, so flies fished in these waters must be ultra-realistic.

Freestone-area tyers, on the other hand, tend to a more impressionistic tie. The Catskill School, for instance, uses a dense collar of top-quality hackle and just a suggestion of wings. The inventors of the Light Cahill and Hendrickson gave away some photographic realism to give their flies a cocky stance on their more turbulent waters.

When buying flies, you too will have to make hard decisions. Which characteristics of a fly are most important to the fish you're casting to? That's one of the questions I hope to help you answer in the following pages.

Dry Flies — Trout

F lies that are designed to float impose the strictest demands on both the tyer's skill and his materials. Every dry fly, since it is tied on a metal hook, starts out heavier than water and will try its darndest to sink—partially or completely.

Therefore the dimensions or proportions (call it style or design, if you like) must be nearly perfect. First, the fly must be aerodynamically balanced so that it will land in an upright, lifelike attitude when it flutters to the surface at the end of a cast. Then it has to exploit surface-tension to the maximum and remain buoyant and jaunty even on choppy water.

But even a perfectly tied fly won't float well unless it is made out of top-quality materials. It is crucial that the hackle-collar at the head and the fibers in the tail are stiff, steely, and allergic to water.

It also helps if the body is water-repellant. If the material wound along the hook shank soaks up water like a sponge, this will make the fly too heavy to float properly. To be truly effective, the standard dry fly for freestone rivers should float high on the water.

Hackle

As you might suppose, the first thing you should look for in a floater is high-quality rooster hackle. Such hackle is stiff and springy. You can check for this by rubbing the fly lightly against one of your lips. If you feel a slight prickly sensation, good. If, on the other hand, the fibers feel as soft as a camel's-hair paintbrush, you're in deep trouble. Quality dry-fly hackle is bristly; it fights back.

A second test is to examine the fly against a strong light-source. If the hackle glints and the tip-ends seem nearly translucent, that's a good sign. If, however, the fibers appear dull or opaque, they're probably second rate. Usually, all the flies in the same compartment have been tied from the same hackle neck, so if two or three samples check out negative, you should consider returning to square one and taking your business elsewhere.

Once you're satisfied with the hackle quality, you can turn your attention to proportion and design. Even though every floater in the bins was probably tied by the same person, no two flies are exactly alike. The best specimens will be a little bit—sometimes even a lot—better than the worst.

The classic mayfly-dun imitation is the end product of years of

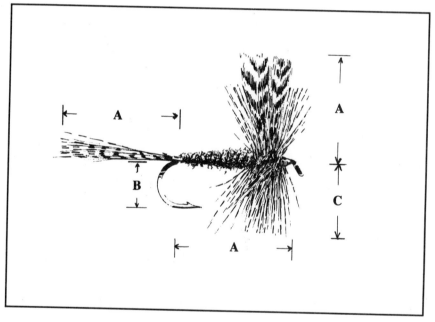

Fig. 2 Mayfly dun showing ideal proportions
A. tail length = wing length = hook-shank length B. hook gape
C. hackle length = 1½ hook gape or ¾ wing length

experimentation and has remained the most popular type of floating trout fly for over a century. Its ideal proportions are shown in Figure 2.

Hackle-Collar

The amount of hackle wound near the wings, its bushyness or sparseness, is a matter of personal taste. Anglers who concentrate on fast-water spate streams often prefer a fairly heavily hackled fly because it will float higher and longer on choppy water. On the other hand, those who fish mainly on placid limestoners usually choose sparser ties. Flotation is less of a problem on calm surfaces; and here, trout get a longer time to inspect a fly so realism (after all, a live mayfly has only six legs) becomes a more important factor.

Tails

Tails, on the other hand, should be rather substantial on all but the tiniest patterns because these few long fibers are called upon to do Herculean work. First, they must create enough wind-resistance, as the fly flutters down to the surface, so that the fly will alight with the hook shank nearly horizontal. This is a demanding task considering all that bushy wound hackle at the other end of the hook. Second, the tail must get a strong grip on surface-tension to keep the heavier end of the hook from sinking during a long float. I know mayflies have only two or three tails (though I'm convinced trout *don't*), but wimpy, skimpy tails just aren't up to the flotation task.

Best of all, of course, are flies whose tails are splayed into two or three small clumps or at least flared in a horizontal plane (see Figures 3 and 4). For some reason, these are extremely hard to find. But, even in a batch of conventionally-tailed flies, you'll find the odd one with some natural or accidental flaring. Pounce on it!

Bodies

Bodies are the least of your worries, but they should be trim and smoothly tapered. Those made of quill—whether stripped peacock

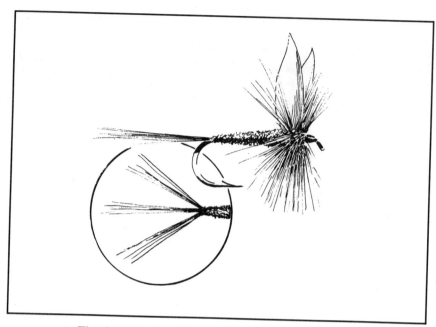

Fig. 3 Tail splayed into two or three clumps . . .

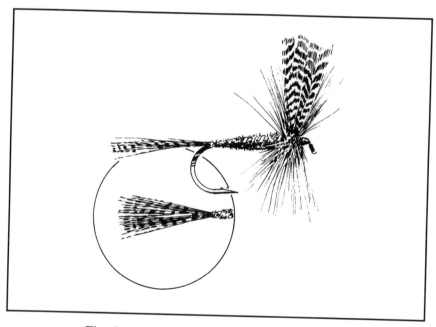

Fig. 4 or at least flared into a horizontal plane

quill or hackle stem—don't absorb water or change color when wet. On the other hand, they are opaque and lack the translucent quality of mayfly abdomens.

Most herls used for bodies—such as pheasant tail and heron—keep their color well when wet and allow light to pass through their fine, short fibers. Unfortunately, there are very few common herls in the paler shades. Then, too, most herls are rather fragile and should be lightly counter-wound with the finest gold wire for protection.

Clipped deer-hair bodies on the famous Irresistible and Rat-Faced McDougal patterns are extremely buoyant—at least for a while. Look for neat tapering and examine them closely to make sure that the hair has been tightly packed, leaving no bald spots.

Silk floss is a favorite with many professionals because it's so easy to handle, but it has several drawbacks. It darkens when wet, absorbs water readily, and is quite fragile. However, some popular patterns like the Royal Coachman and Pink Lady call for floss and you can't avoid it.

The most common type of dry-fly bodies—those dubbed with fur or some synthetic substitute—can present problems, especially in the larger, harder-to-float sizes. Here, you'll have to ask the tyer what materials he used. Wool yarn soaks up water like a sponge. Most furs of aquatic animals—notably seal—shed water well. Synthetics are a mixed lot. Polypropylene, first introduced on the Swisher-Richards no-hackle flies, is lighter than water and will float well if properly annointed. Whatever the material, look for bodies with the bare minimum of dubbing—just enough to give the desired color and to hide the hook shank.

Dubbing color can be deceptive. What you see in the shop is not necessarily what the trout will see on the stream. Many materials darken—a few actually change color—when wet and this is especially true of the palest shades. Seal's fur is quite stable while pale fox belly darkens more than I like. Poly is acceptable. Shiny Antron is even better, but it's so hard to spin that you're not likely to find it on many dries.

You could check for color-fastness with a drop of spit on your index finger, but the proprietor might not appreciate this too much—especially during flu season. It's wiser to inquire about body materials.

Wings

Wings deserve more than casual scrutiny. Whether made of hair, plumage, hackle feathers, or slips of quill, they should be positioned dead-center on top of the hook and each of the wings should be of the same size, length, and bushyness. These are usually separated from each other at an angle of from 30 to 60 degrees. Anything within that range is acceptable as long as both wings veer away from the vertical at the same angle. Wings made from slips of primary wing quills need to pass a further test. They must be perfectly aligned along the longitudinal axis of the fly (see Figure 5) or they'll twist a fine tippet like the rubber band inside a model airplane.

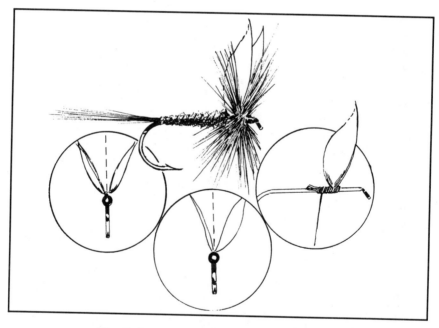

Fig. 5 Quill wing placement and alignment

Patterns and Colors

While no two of the hundreds of North American mayfly species look exactly alike, all are remarkably similar in shape and most fit into a few basic color schemes. The colors are cream, ginger, brown-and-grizzly, medium dun, and dark dun with olive body. For the creams, the popular Light Cahill covers a lot of territory and you should have sizes #14, #16, and #18. The Ginger Quill is a good choice for the light-brown flies and should be carried in the same sizes recommended above. The Adams is a great mixed-hackle fly and I'd suggest sizes #12, #14, and #16. Either the Quill Gordon or the Hendrickson will cover the medium-dun flies and here I'd like to have #12s, #14s, #16s, and #18s. Then get some dark Blue-Winged Olives in sizes #14, #16, and #18.

Of course, you'll rarely be matching the hatch precisely with such a skeletal selection and I know you'll want to add to this cadre. By all means pick up some local favorites when you're away from home territory. Each region seems to have a few "strange beasts" like huge brown *Hexagenias* or tiny #24 Tricos. But the recommended selection will at least keep you in the ball game over 90 percent of the time when duns are hatching.

How many of each size and pattern should you carry with you? I'd suggest a minimum of three. That would let you leave one in a fish or a tree, cast the second until it got soggy or chewed up, and you'd still be in business with your third. However, if you fish an area where, say, small sulphurs hatch out every evening for two months or so, you might want a whole boxful of the most successful pattern.

No-hackle dries and Comparaduns have become popular recently—especially on placid slow-water streams (see Figure 6). They have proved most effective in sizes #16 and smaller because, even on calm water, surface tension won't support a larger hook for long without the help of hackle.

Since such flies usually have full, prominent wings, make sure they're set symmetrically so that the fly won't spin like a propellor during casting. Tails should be split and widely separated, otherwise a no-hackle is likely to fall over on its side once it hits the water.

13

Fig. 6 No-Hackle fly

If you never, or rarely, fish spring creeks or limestoners, you may feel you don't need any no-hackles, but I'd recommend you carry a few #16s, #18s, and #20s in both pale yellow and blue-winged olive patterns. These are common colors for small mayflies and even freestone trout can get quite choosy when they're feeding in long, slow flats or pools. Those who fish limestone-type streams regularly would do well to carry at least the basic color schemes suggested for standards and in all the above sizes.

Since these flies become nearly useless once their bodies get soggy, five or six of each are none too many. No-hackles can be recycled reasonably quickly on sunny, breezy days, but late in the evening or during damp weather you may well be limited to one fish per fly.

Parachute-tied dry flies are essentially no-hackle flies with a sparse hackle wound horizontally around the base of the wings (see

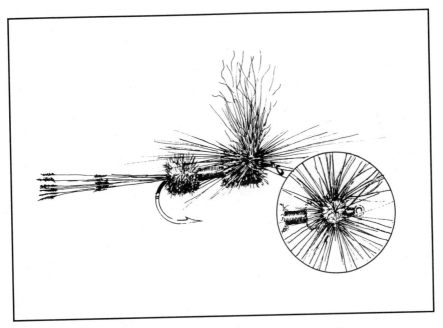

Fig. 7 Parachute fly with top view detail

Figure 7). Since this puts the hackle-fibers above the hook shank, they can't play any part in floating the body of the fly, but act as outriggers, helping the imitation to ride wings-up.

I doubt that even the fussiest dry-fly man needs both parachutes and no-hackles in all the same sizes and colors. I'd suggest you try some of one type and some of the other, then make up your final selection out of the style that pleases you—or, rather, the trout you pursue—most.

Thorax flies originated in Pennsylvania's limestone country and occupy a niche somewhere between standard and no-hackle dries (see Figure 8). This type of fly floats well in sizes up to #12, so it can be used to imitate many of the larger (but not the largest) freestone-stream insects. It gains a step in realism over standard ties because the hackling is less dense; and since the body is supported above the water surface, it seems to gain a point over the

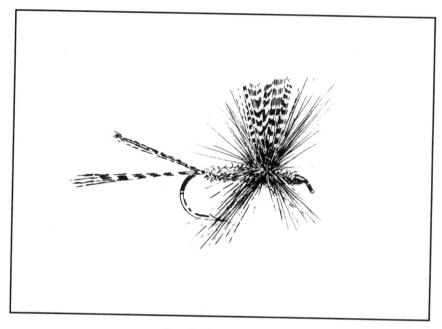

Fig. 8 Thorax fly

no-hackles.

Why this style of dressing never really caught on, I can't explain. Perhaps it looks ugly to fishermen even though it doesn't to trout. Or maybe professionals find it more demanding to tie. In any event, thorax flies are hard to find.

Check the points I suggested for no-hackles—well-split tails, symmetrical wings—but also test for hackle-quality and make sure the hackle sloping to the rear is longer than the forward one. This will slant the tail slightly upward—as the inventor, the late Vince Marinaro, intended.

All in all, this tie is probably most useful for picky, slow-water trout. Try a few in the same colors and sizes as your no-hackles or parachutes and you just might end up with all thoraxes. It's the most durable of the three ties and an individual fly should be able to take several fish without requiring change.

Variants

I'd feel only half-equipped if I stepped into any freestone trout water without a few large, bushy variants. They can pound up fish in fast runs and pockets, pull fish up out of still, deep pools (especially if twitched slightly) and they can save the day when a hatch of huge drakes appears unexpectedly. Lastly, they're top-notch floaters and will stay afloat even during a steady drizzle.

Variants are merely big, wingless, standard dry flies tied on small hooks. Hackle radius should measure about three hook gapes instead of the standard one-and-a-half and, to balance out the fly, tails should be nearly twice normal length (see Figure 9).

Hackle quality is pivotal to a variant's effectiveness. The higher these flies sit on the water, the better. Meticulous tyers use

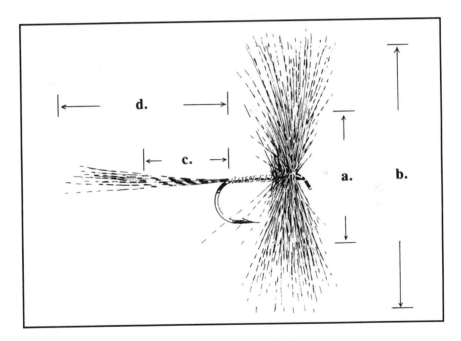

Fig. 9 Dimensions for a Standard Dry Fly and Variant
a. Standard hackle length   b. Variant hackle length
c. Standard tail length   d. Variant tail length

only spade hackles—those short, extra-long-fibered feathers on the very edge of mature rooster capes—for variants. There are never many of these on any one bird and some birds have none at all. Check hackle stiffness with the same criteria recommended for standard dries. When, or if, you find a batch of variants with exceptional hackles, stock up. They're as scarce as roosters' teeth.

Some professionals tie variants on short-shanked hooks (see Figures 10 and 11), others on standard lengths. I prefer the latter because the weight is not that much greater and I feel they have superior hooking qualities.

Hook size tells you little about the actual bulk of these patterns so I'll suggest you select them by the diameter of their throat hackle. The smallest you'll need will be about one inch across and the biggest you'll want to cast will run about two inches. The smaller ones should be on #16 hooks (#18s don't hook well with all that guarding hackle) and the largest shouldn't be asked to

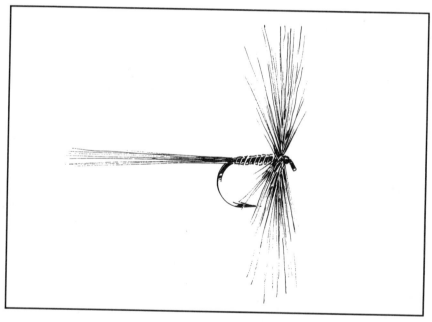

Fig. 10 Variant on short-shank hook

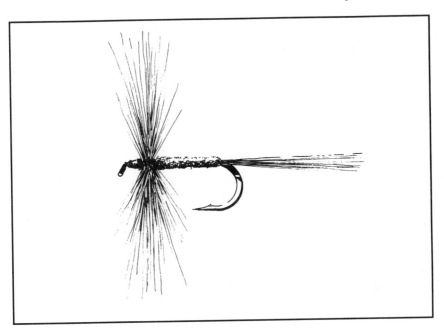

Fig. 11 Variant on standard hook

carry a hook bigger than #12.

Since variants are exciter flies rather than exact imitations, a few colors will suffice. Art Flick recommended only three: cream, ginger-and-grizzly, and medium dun. I've never felt any need to add to this list, but I carry three sizes of each and three of each size for the same reasons I mentioned for mayfly patterns.

Spinners

I can't understand why so many good fishermen don't have any spent-wing patterns in their boxes. Often trout will accept no substitutes—especially on late-spring and summer evenings. During that last half-hour of daylight when trout start sipping "invisible" flies on flats and pools, spent-wing mayflies are the main course nine times out of ten. The better class of trout can spot the differences between a dun and a spinner silhouette without benefit of bifocals every time.

19

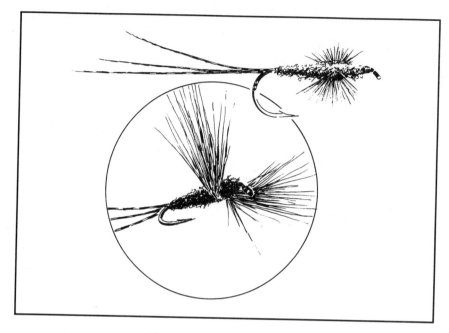

Fig. 12 Marinaro spinner

Nearly all spinners have gauzy, transparent wings; for this reason, opaque materials make poor wing imitations. Far too many spent-wing patterns are winged with bucktail, impala, or polypropylene, which are both dense and chalky-white.

The late Vince Marinaro was a stickler on spinners. He maintained that the key characteristic of a natural on the water was the sparkles of condensed light created by the folds and veins of the wings. The best way to recreate this, he claimed, was with fine, well-spaced hackle fibers that would crinkle the water into a series of prisms. I'm convinced he was right. Look for spinner imitations with horizontal clumps of hackle fibers. Palest dun is the best if you can find it.

Spinners have even slimmer bodies than duns and much longer tails, so look for these traits in artificials. Trout will. Trim, quill bodies are excellent for these patterns. You almost always fish this type of fly at dusk when all the trout can see is the silhouette—

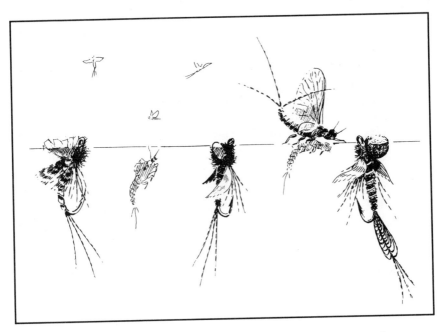

Fig. 13, 14, 15 Emerger patterns—feather tuft, small cork, flotant in silk stocking . . .

so translucency is not important (see Figure 12).

I've never felt the need for more than two patterns because color is less of a factor in near-darkness. One has a red-brown body with palest-dun hackle and the other a yellow body with pale-cream wings. Sizes #14, #16, and #18 are most useful and a couple of each should be plenty. After all, if you leave a fly in a fish, you're lucky to have enough light, when the bats are flying, to tie on another.

Emergers

I don't know whether or not these are true dry flies (Halford would certainly have banned them), but I do know they're indispensable at times. They imitate mayfly duns that have hit the surface film and are either stuck there or are just starting to hatch out.

These artificials look much like nymphs, but there are two important differences. Emergers should be tied on light-wire hooks so they won't sink. And they sport a set of small, unfurling wings instead of a flattened wing case (see Figures 13, 14, 15).

These embryo wings can be represented by a short tuft of feathers, a painted oval of cork, or some floating material encased in a small bag of silk-stocking material. I have a fondness for the latter two types because the floating wing-materials assure that the fly will stay on, or just under, the surface film.

Look for the same qualities in these flies that you would in true nymphs and it's wise to carry patterns in the same sizes and colors. (See chapter "Nymphs.") These are durable flies, but it pays to carry two of each, just in case.

Caddis

Although imitations of adult caddisflies have become increasingly available, many anglers don't carry any of these floaters. That's

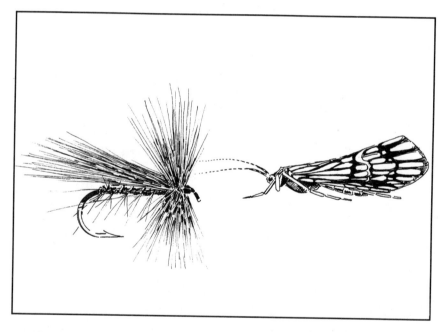

Fig. 16 . . . caddis wings are not upright but are folded, tent-like, in an inverted "V" along the body.

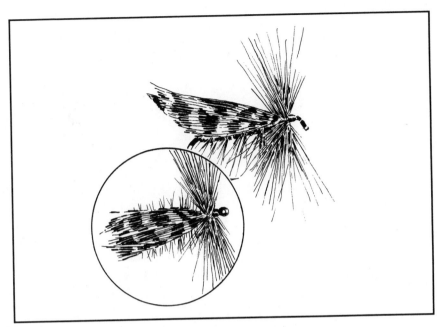

Fig. 17 . . . a good imitation should capture these qualities.

short-sighted because caddisflies are extremely abundant and are nearly as important a trout food as mayflies are. When educated trout are slashing at caddis, they'll rarely fall for a mayfly imitation because the shape of a caddis is totally different.

Caddis wings are not held upright, but are folded, tentlike, in an inverted "V" along the body (see Figure 16). Then, too, caddisflies—wings and all—are nearly opaque while most mayflies are distinctly translucent. A good imitation should capture these qualities (see Figure 17).

Elk-Hair Caddis

The most popular and available floating imitation is the elk-hair caddis (see Figure 18). This fly is durable, buoyant, and a good imitation of the many brown or mottled-brown species. However, some of the biggest caddis hatches are made up of flies whose color can't even be approximated with elk hair.

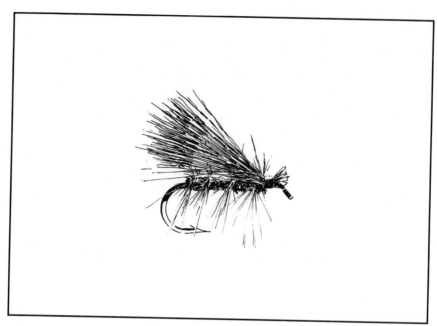

Fig. 18 Elk-Hair Caddis

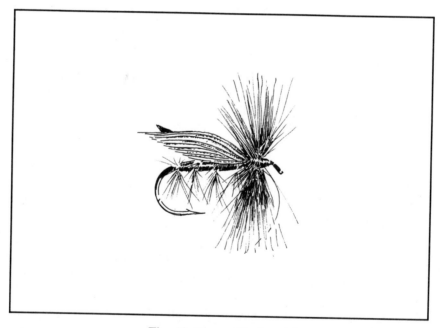

Fig. 19 Henryville Special

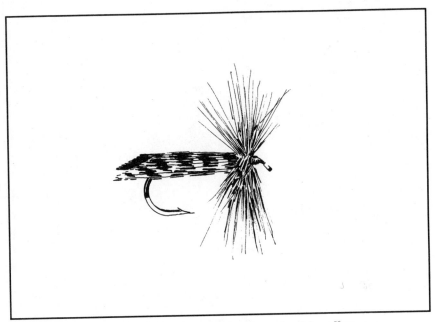

Fig. 20 Clipped-to-shape wing—hackle collar

Henryville

Another style, the Henryville, has a palmer-hackled body to aid flotation and two slips of primary quill to suggest wings (see Figure 19). This is a good floater and looks caddisy enough if the wings are tied flat to the body, but the wings are quite fragile. A third style presents a caddislike silhouette with a flat, clipped-to-shape feather for a wing and a hackle-collar at the head (see Figure 20). This can be killing on slow, glassy water, but it's only a so-so floater and not much use on fast runs or pocket water.

Fluttering Caddis

The best all-around design, I'm convinced, is winged with a bunch of stiff hackle or mink-tail fibers with a generous hackle-collar at the head (see Figure 21). This is an amazingly tough fly that will

25

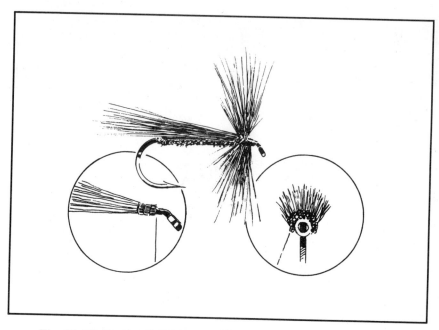

Fig. 21 Fluttering Caddis with detail of proper wing alignment

outfloat a variant, catch fish after fish without getting soggy, and stay on top even during a steady rain. It presents a realistic imitation whether viewed from the side or from below, and it fools fish on all types of water. A few tyers and shops sell this type of caddis and it's well worth looking for.

Hackle quality is important for top performance and you should check it as suggested for mayfly duns. Fiber wings—whether elk hair, hackle-fiber, or mink tail—should encircle the top half of the body, filling an arc of 180 degrees or a bit more, and should hug the body, tightly (see Figure 21).

Patterns and Colors

Caddis come in many sizes and colors, but you can fool most caddis-feeding trout with a few good, general patterns. I'd recommend imitations in the following colors: medium dun, light dun, brown,

brown-and-grizzly, ginger, and palest ginger. Sizes #14, #16, and #18 should cover the majority of the hatches you'll encounter.

Since both the Henryville and flat-winged patterns are fairly fragile and not the best of floaters, you should carry three of each color and size. However, a couple each of the fiber-winged models should see you through.

Stone Flies

These are needed only occasionally in their adult, flying form—more often in the West than in the East. Most species crawl out onto shore to hatch and fly off out of the fish's reach. However, it's good insurance to carry a few patterns just in case. Since most of the common, smaller species are yellow or yellow-brown, I carry a few in that color range on size #14 and #16 hooks. When tied up much like the fiber-winged caddis with pale-dun wings, they look like the real thing on the water. Such flies, however, are rarely stock items so, if stone flies are important on your waters, you may have to get them custom tied.

There is one regional fly that I'll touch on because it is important over a large area. Hatches of the huge stone fly called the Salmon Fly are a major annual event on many western rivers. Like the Mayfly of Europe, this oversized insect gives dry-fly anglers a shot at large fish that otherwise rarely take surface food.

Some of the best-known imitations are the Sofa Pillow, Bird's Stone Fly, and the Henry's Fork Stone Fly (see Figure 22). Since the naturals are most abundant on fast-water stretches, flotability is crucial. Since the artificials are usually tied on monstrous size #6 hooks, look for top-quality hackle and lots of it.

Terrestrials

Since up to 40 percent of the trout's summer food is made up of accidental, land-bred flies, imitations of these windfalls shouldn't be neglected. The most common of these are ants, beetles, and grasshoppers. I have no idea which of these insects is most prevalent in your area, but I do know that trout have a pronounced fondness for ants.

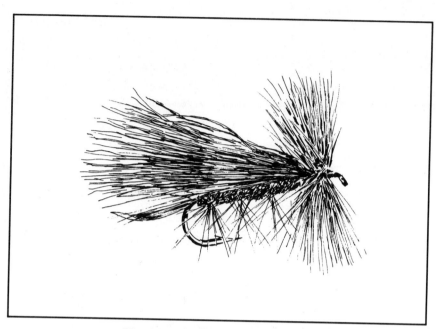

Fig. 22 Stoneflies   a. Sofa Pillow

b. Bird's Stonefly

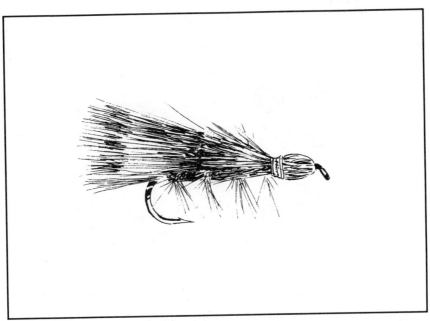

c. Henry's Fork Stone Fly

Ants

These come in a variety of colors, but the two most common are jet-black and cinnamon or ginger. Good patterns can be tied up out of a variety of materials—cork, horse hair, deer hair, and any number of herls and dubbings.

Whatever the materials used, the design of the pattern may be the most important factor. Ants have a distinctive silhouette. All have a large oval abdomen separated from the smaller thorax and head by a wasp waist (see Figure 23). Make sure the ones you select emphasize this hourglass figure because I'm convinced trout key in on this characteristic.

I prefer ants with a shiny, lacquered finish because they look to me more like the real McCoy, but I'm not sure trout are all that picky. I carry blacks in sizes #12, #14, and #16 and cinnamons in

Fig. 23 Different styles of ants showing hourglass shape

#14, #16, and #18 because most of this color run smallish. Happily, excellent hackle is not important here because these flies should float soggily, awash in the surface film.

Beetles

Beetles plop into the water regularly and are welcomed by trout though I've never encountered a concentration or "hatch" of any one species. I carry only one imitation; it is black because that's the most common beetle color. Like ants, beetles lie low in the water and can be made out of any number of materials that will float or just barely. Sizes #10, #12, and #14 seem to cover most bases.

Grasshoppers

Grasshoppers make a big mouthful and are popular with trout—

Fig. 24 Types of Hoppers   a. Tail-hair

especially during late summer. I find an imitation killing even on woodland streams where I rarely see a natural. Perhaps it is a dual-purpose fly and the trout mistake it for a giant stone fly.

Artificial grasshoppers can be tied up in a number of styles, but their one common denominator is a large, succulent body that's usually yellow. This can be made up out of all kinds of materials including painted cork or balsa wood and clipped, dyed deer hair. If the body materials used are not naturally buoyant, they should be annointed liberally with a first-rate floatant before use.

Wings can be as simple as mottled brown tail-hair tied generously on the top half of the fly (see Figure 24a). Many popular patterns use speckled turkey for wings plus a brown-and-grizzly hackle-collar up front (see Figure 24b). The fanciest imitations add large "jumper" legs of hackle stems on each side, as well (see Figure 24c).

Which type should you use?

24b. Turkey wing with hackle-collar

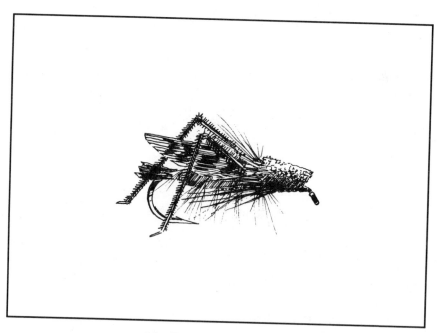

24c. Exact imitation/legs

Fairly simple patterns like the time-tested Joe's Hopper do well in most places—especially fast, broken water. But if you find yourself in calmer water, or an area where almost every angler is splatting out hoppers, you might gain an edge with the most realistic design like the Jay-Dave, with its down-protruding legs.

I like hoppers that run from an inch up to an inch-and-a-half in overall length. It's wise to carry four or five of each size because this dry often raises trout of leader-breaking dimensions.

Dry Flies—
Salmon

4

E verything I said about the importance of high-quality hackle
to the performance of trout dries goes double for salmon
floaters. Even the special, light-wire, Wilson hooks usually used
are several times as heavy as the average trout-fly hook. Hook-
weight increases far more rapidly as flies get larger than does the
area of surface-tension the hackle can exploit.

On top of this, even the most expensive dry-fly necks—those
that tie up into steely-hackled trout patterns—begin to show a flab-
biness of feather when their hackle-barbs get more than an inch
long. Ideally, spade hackles—those short, wide feathers on the
very edges of some capes—should be used for salmon dries. However, there aren't very many of these on any one neck (none on
some) and they're also needed for variants and tails of trout dries.
I don't want to sound like the voice of doom and gloom, but even
the choicest salmon floaters are none too buoyant.

Fortunately, few salmon flies use hackle fibers for tails. Deer
hair or calf tail are the most common materials and these are usually applied generously enough for good flotation at the rear of the
fly. These are also the most common winging materials. (See Figures 25 and 26.) Check wings for symmetry as you would a trout
fly. Bodies seldom pose problems, but should be trim and
smoothly tapered. Actually, first-rate long hackle is such a rarity
that I'm not too picky about the rest of the fly if the throat hackle
looks top-notch.

Since salmon dries make no attempt to match the hatch (if
any) you won't need many patterns. I know highly successful anglers who have used only one pattern—though in several sizes—
for years. If you carry two each of the Hairwing Royal Coachman,

Fig. 25 Salmon dry showing deer winging and tailing

White Wulff, and brown and grey bivisibles in sizes #8, #6, and #4 you'll be pretty well covered.

Bombers

However, there is another type of dry that looks entirely different—and this too should be in your box. This is the clipped-deer-hair-bodied Bomber that is not intended to ride high but rather float awash like a small log (see Figure 27). Why salmon take this "bass bug" so regularly, I have no idea. Some days they'll grab it while it's dragging—really skittering—across the pool-surface at the end of a float.

I don't know anyone who pretends to be a connoisseur of these creations. All have a similar clipped-deer-hair body. Some have tufts of white calf-tail at both ends and some don't. Often the traditional brown hackle that's wound palmer-style up the body is

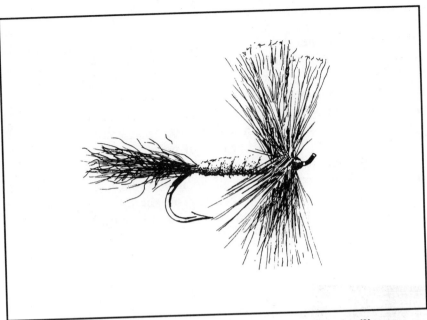

Fig. 26 Salmon dry showing calf tail winging and tailing

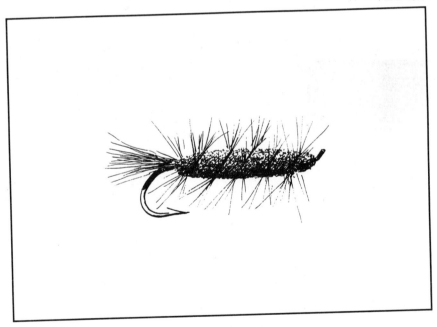

Fig. 27 Bomber

changed to another color, but I don't think these variations make much difference. A Bomber is a Bomber is a Bomber.

The main thing I look for in this type of fly is hook-clearance. Since the chunky body is wound on a long-shank hook, the remaining bite can get skimpy. Enveigling a salmon into taking your fly is no longer such a common occurrence that you'll want to risk merely scratching the fish because of greatly reduced hook-bite.

Hook size tells you little about the actual dimensions of Bombers. Small ones are about an inch-and-a-half long and the biggies will stretch to three inches. You should be equipped with several sizes and two of each should be sufficient.

Wet Flies

5

The wet fly was the original insect imitation and is centuries older than dry flies or nymphs. Early wet flies were dapped and danced on the water with long rods as well as fished underwater. Modern anglers tend to look upon wets as Stone Age lures—fit only to fool wilderness brook trout. Yet, long before the Pilgrims landed, these flies had proved themselves on the wary brown trout of Europe and, if we can believe the old books, huge baskets of trout were killed on them.

Today, the wet fly has been largely replaced in America by the newer, more "scientific" nymph. This is a shame because the wet fly, in one of its many forms, can do almost everything a nymph can do and a lot of things a nymph can't. The spate of recent angler-entomologists seem to have hooked us on "exact imitation" and we've relegated the wet fly to near-museum status.

One of the great, forgotten virtues of the wet fly is that wings and hackle breathe and kick in the water, giving them an extra aliveness that few nymphs possess. Then, too, when danced in and out of the surface film on a dropper, wet flies—especially all-hackle patterns—open up and close down like tiny octopuses. Trout find this nearly irresistible. Experts who fish for brown and sea trout on the lakes of Scotland and Ireland wouldn't be caught dead fishing a corpselike nymph. And I can count on the toes of one foot the number of Atlantic salmon anglers I know who've ever given nymphs a try.

Conventional, Winged Trout Flies

Casting a sunk fly (or team of flies) across, or across and downstream, has caught more trout than all the other presentations combined. One reason for this is that this technique covers so much more water and, for this type of fishing, the classic wet fly is the lure without peer. Hackle, or hackle and wings, pulsate in the current provocatively while the wing helps to keel the fly, hook-downward. This steady position usually means that a fish is hooked either in the secure lower jaw or in the scissors rather than in the hard roof of the mouth. A nymph, on the other hand, has little life of its own and tends to wobble, or even rotate, as it swings through the current—and you never know whether its hook is pointing up, down, or sideways.

Many modern anglers shun the standard wet fly because they consider it a nondescript lure rather than a working imitation of some specific life-form. I think that bias presupposes too much anatomical analysis by the trout's minute brain. I have every reason to doubt that trout add up body segments and count legs before taking, or refusing, our offerings.

I can think of many kinds of specific trout foods that certain wet flies imitate effectively. The Greenwell's Glory is a cracking imitation of our Quill Gordon, which hatches out on the stream-bottom and rises to the surface as a winged fly. The popular Hare's Ear offers more than a passing likeness to sow bugs, shrimps, and many emerging caddis pupae. The old Black Gnat may well be taken for a drowned land beetle and the pale Pink Lady for a spent mayfly that has been tumbled underwater in the rapids. Small silver-bodied wets can double as either tiny minnow fry or the many types of caddisflies that take a sparkling bubble of air down with them when egg-laying underwater. And wets with mottled, plumage wings of wood duck or bronze mallard—the Light Cahill is a good example—offer a superb likeness to many common mayfly nymphs.

Then there are time-tested flies like the Royal Coachman and the Rio Grande King that seem to be pure fancies; yet they catch lots of trout, year in, year out. I have a devout fondness for flies that kill a lot of fish, whether or not I have the wit to figure out what the trout mistake them for.

When selecting individual wet flies, give preference to those

Fig. 28 Wet-fly proportions

with small, neat heads. This gives sunk flies a neat entry and good swimming characteristics. Wings should be equal in size and properly centered on the hook shank (see Figure 28). And they should lie close along the top of the body, enveloping the top half of it so that they appear like the mottled, darker top of a nymph's body.

Let your choice err on the side of the sparser ties. Most wets have far too much wing and hackle. Hackle tips should not reach the point of the hook, and the fewer their number, the better the fly will keel. Don't make the mistake of feeling that you need bulky feathers to catch a trout's eye. They can see, and feed on, minute organisms. *More* is seldom better; give the trout as little as possible to find fault with.

Patterns

A spartan, minimum selection of wets should include Light Cahills,

41

March Browns, Hare's Ears, Leadwing Coachmen, Black Gnats, and dark Greenwell's Glories. These will pretty well cover the basic color ranges of most mayflies and caddises. However, you should include one or two attractor patterns like the Royal Coachman or Rio Grande King and one silver-bodied pattern as well. These should be in sizes #10, #12, and #14, while the drabber, more imitative patterns should run from sizes #12 through #16.

Since wet-fly leaders are usually heavier than those used for dry flies, you shouldn't decorate too many fish-mouths with your offerings. And there's no need to change to a new wet fly after catching a fish. Wets seem to get more effective as they grow soggier and more chewed-up. Two of each pattern and size should see you through even the best of days.

All-Hackle Wets

Wet flies without wings—not to be confused with true nymphs—are still enormously popular in the British Isles even though they're seldom used here in America. The Brown-Hackle Peacock and the Grey-Hackle Yellow were among the most popular patterns before World War II, yet I haven't seen either one in a tackle store for decades. I guess they're too "unrealistic" for today's sophisticated fly fishers.

Hackle-only wets fall into three main categories: those with shoulder poultry-hackle only, those with palmer-hackled bodies as well as shoulder-hackle, and those with only a turn or two of soft plumage feathers. All seem to have originated in Europe many centuries ago and were among the standard fly-types used in early American and Canadian trout fishing. (See Figure 29.)

I'll admit that such flies would not be my first choice for spring creeks and limestoners. Floating flies are overwhelming favorites on such placid waters and even "exact-imitation" nymphs run dries a poor second on these streams.

But the vast majority of our flowing trout waters are rain-fed spate streams with runs, rapids, riffles, and pockets. In these braided and boiling currents, a fly with an extra life of its own can be deadly. Fish are rarely selective in these less-fertile streams and trout have to be opportunistic to make a living. A fly that appears to struggle and kick is off to a big head-start here.

Such flies are fortunately less demanding on a tyer's skill and his materials. I check for a neat head, smoothly tapered body, and sparse hackling.

Since these patterns are impressionistic, only the basic colors need be covered. A yellow body with buff hackle, a tan body with ginger hackle, a brown body hackled with brown-and-grizzly-mixed, and an all-dun fly seem to cover a lot of territory, but I'm extremely partial to flies with olive and green bodies with either a woodcock or brown partridge hackle at the head. Sizes #10, #12, and #14 are most useful, I've found.

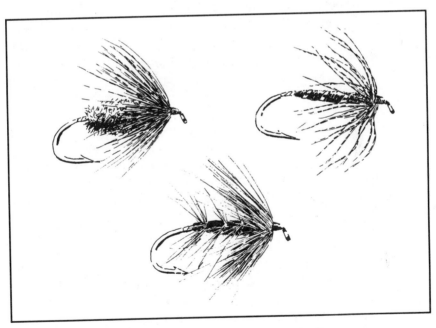

Fig. 29 Three types of all-hackle wet flies

Salmon Flies

The classic (or near-classic) wet salmon fly is, I'm happy to report, alive and well on nearly all Atlantic salmon rivers. The dry fly may have gained popularity on Canadian waters, but, even here, it is considered a special weapon for warm, low-water conditions or a rolling fish that won't come to a standard wet. In Europe and Iceland, where cooler waters prevail, the dry fly is rarely used; and even in Canada it is seldom employed for random prospecting because it covers so little water.

Classic Salmon Patterns

On big, deep rivers, where larger flies are called for, those beautiful, fully-dressed Jock Scotts, Silver Doctors, Green Highlanders, and the like are still popular. However, since there are nearly thirty different feathers, or slips of feathers, in the wing of a proper Jock Scott, the fly-dresser has to omit some of this plumage on flies #6 or smaller to keep the fly from becoming grotesque. This has led to further simplification of patterns by substituting hair of one or several colors for the complex plumage wing.

Bugs

Experimentation during the last twenty-five years or so has shown that Atlantics have a greater catholicity of taste than nineteenth-century anglers ever dreamed of. Clipped deer-hair "Buck Bugs" have proved extremely effective on some rivers even though they differ widely in shape and silhouette from the old standbys. Muddlers and similar tadpole-shaped patterns are rising in popularity, too.

Because of this trend, salmon flies have become easier to tie, and the necessary materials are less expensive. This, I feel, is only a tiny step forward. Salmon fishing is usually expensive—often damnably so—and the price of flies is a minute fraction of the overall cost. A hairwing or a "bug" may be twenty-five to fifty cents cheaper than a fully-dressed classic, but since I haven't lost a single salmon fly in the last few years, I can't consider this a major economy. This may sound stuffy, but I feel that running a deer-hair "Green Machine" down a salmon pool instead of a plumage-winged Green Highlander is like renting a pricey grouse moor in Scotland and then economizing by banging away at the driven birds with a cheap pump gun.

Proportions

The things to look for when buying classic patterns—even the smaller, reduced models—are overall proportions and symmetry of wings. Figure 30 illustrates what a leading authority, Pryce-Tannatt, considered the perfect fly and I can only add "Amen." Check the wings from both sides and several angles. Make sure they're properly centered, equal in size, and that all major plumage feathers get an equal showing on both sides. In smaller sizes, there's often a tendency toward too much and too-long

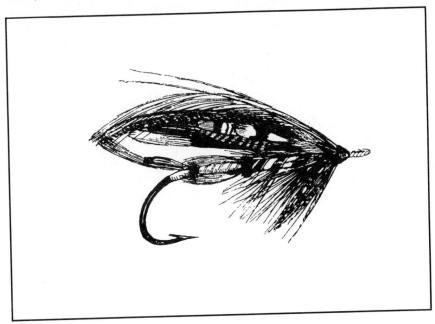

Fig. 30 Atlantic salmon fly—per Pryce Tannatt

hackle. Let the illustration guide you as to proper wing and hackle lengths. For hairwings, your inspection/selection standards should be much the same. Above all, make sure the fly or flies you pick will swim well without wobbling and with the hook-point straight down where it will engage the fish's more secure lower jaw or scissors.

With clipped deer-hair bug patterns you can never be sure a fly will keel properly because they're all tied in the round. Do make sure, though, that there's enough gape left between hook-point and bulky body to ensure a firm bite.

Patterns

Which sizes and patterns should you carry? Collecting fancy salmon flies is like eating salted peanuts: it's nearly impossible to stop. We tend to buy and carry far more than we need or ever use.

An abstemious selection should include a nearly all-black fly like the Nighthawk or Mitchell, a medium black like the Jock Scott or Black Dose, a silver body like the Silver Grey or Silver Doctor, and a green-and-yellow for high, colored water like the Green Highlander or Cosseboom. Sizes #6, #8, and #10 are most useful for summer fishing, but carry a few #4s in the brighter sizes in case of high water. (Of course, if you're privileged to fish the big, expensive rivers in June, you'll need flies a lot bigger.)

With the bug series, the natural brown models with both green and red butts are popular. So is the all-green Green Machine and a newcomer, the all-blue (you guessed it) Blue Machine. However, you may not need to stock up on these because, on most rivers, your guide will have a boxful and he'll plead and whine until you let him tie one on.

Hooks

Doubles or singles, that is the question. In the smaller sizes, I strongly favor flies tied on lightweight, low-water doubles. These keel more surely than small singles and I'm convinced (and so is Lee Wulff) that they give a more secure hold on fish. The same can be said for doubles in the larger sizes and, being considerably heavier, (you can't use lead or split shot on salmon rivers) they tend to ride underwater rather than furrowing the surface film in fast June currents. However, #3/0 doubles are brutes to cast and you may want to scale down to singles in the heavyweight division.

Warmwater Wets

Big, bright wet flies used to be the most popular fly-rod lures for bass, but streamers and bass bugs have almost completely taken over this market. It's not that bass don't like wet flies anymore. I've caught hundreds on medium-sized Jock Scotts and Durham Rangers. But you probably can't find true bass wet flies anymore so that's one set of flies you won't have to buy.

Panfish are another matter. Except for still evenings, wets will catch more perch and sunfish than floaters will. Mature specimens of these species are none too big, so, if you use too small a fly

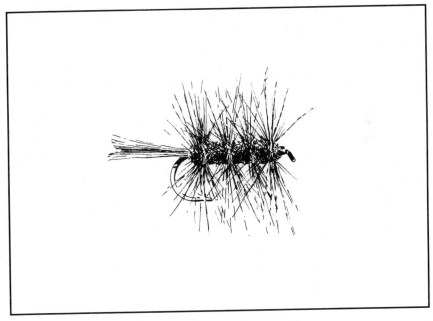

Fig. 31a. Wooly Worm

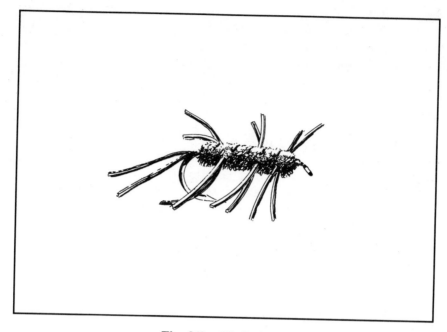

Fig. 31b. Girdle Bug

you'll be pestered by juveniles. I use size #10s most of the time.

Woolly worms and girdle bugs (see Figure 31)—flies with lively, built-in action—are excellent when retrieved with slow twitches. So are many of the old, wet patterns that are now considered too bright and gaudy for trout. I've found the McGinty especially murderous. And the old Black Gnat is hard to beat.

Nymphs

6

True nymph fishing—representing a dislodged or hatching mayfly nymph in realistic manner with a special fly—is a relatively recent technique. Of course, some fly fishers had discovered, centuries ago, that an old, beat-up wet fly that had shed its wings was often more effective than a new, fully dressed one. Others had also recommended fishing the sunk fly upstream. But it wasn't until G. E. M. Skues published *Minor Tactics of the Chalk Stream* in 1910 that the world at large learned how to tie and present this more realistic representation of underwater insects.

Mayfly Imitations

Nymphs are primarily trout lures. They'll also take many other types of fish, but they never gained much popularity as bass or panfish flies (though recently they've become popular for smallmouth bass in rivers). The late Charlie Defeo spent years working on a series of Atlantic salmon nymphs for low-water fishing, yet these didn't catch on, either.

Traditionally, nymphs are fished differently from wet flies. They are most effective when cast upstream and allowed to sink down nearer the trout's eye level on a natural, dry-fly-like dead drift. With this presentation, a skilled angler can often catch fish that are off their feed and not in the least bit interested in rising up out of their lies to take a dry or even a wet.

Upstream nymphing, when practiced by an expert, can produce good catches when all other methods are drawing blanks. But getting an artificial nymph to travel naturally near the stream bottom and then detecting the subtle takes on a slack line are no easy tasks. In fact, this is by far the most difficult, demanding, and—some say—excruciating form of our gentle art.

Of course, nymph imitations are also deadly during the early stages of a hatch when rising nymphs outnumber the few duns already floating on top. At such times, a nymph fished across-stream, or even across and down like the traditional wet fly, will work well, too.

Since artificial nymphs, in general, are attempts at more exact imitations of the dislodged or hatching natural, some tyers go all the way and put on photographically realistic, lacquered wing cases and exactly six legs, bent in the right places. Such flies do look a lot more like the real thing to you and me, but I feel they're too precious (and expensive) to fish with and deserve to be mounted as exhibits. Trout are neither anatomists nor artists and can be fooled by far simpler, more impressionistic ties.

Several books have been published, in recent years, showing, in color, what many of our more common mayfly nymphs look like from the top. This is a great help in identifying individual nymphs you may capture when overturning rocks in the streambed. But I'm less certain that it helps the fly tyer concoct a better imitation.

The reason for this is that I've never run across either color drawings or photos showing what the *bottom sides* of our nymphs look like when they are alive. What shade is the belly? What color are the gills and how big are they? How much and how rapidly do they move? Photos or drawings of their top sides—and usually from dead, preserved specimens—don't begin to answer these questions. So far, I've had to choose my imitations based on recollections of sample nymphs I've caught in the stream.

And capturing these nymphs has taught me another important lesson. When I let my captives go, I noticed that they all swam down to the stream bottom (though some quicker than others) *right-side* up, even in swift water. So, I reasoned, if dislodged, or hatching, nymphs normally swim this way, then it is their *belly-color* we should be imitating. I'm convinced that 99 times out of 100, a natural mayfly nymph (and our own imitations, as well) will be passing above the fish's head. This means that trout rarely get a look at those beautifully mottled backs and wing cases that the books present to anglers.

Therefore, the nymphs I choose, and recommend, are fairly simple ones, *tied in the round*. By this I mean, bodies and thoraxes that are the same color, top and bottom (see Figure 32). I fully realize that those with darker mottled backs and wing cases appear more realistic when held in the hand. But they probably won't to a fish who sees them passing overhead.

Artificial nymphs are notoriously poor "keelers," spinning and turning in the current and rarely riding with the hook-point straight down. If I want to present a trout with a yellow-bellied nymph like the March Brown, I'll put on a nymph with a body that's the same color, top or bottom. That way, no matter how my imitation twists or turns, it will always show the fish that tell-tale yellow color.

Although trout will, for some reason, often hold a dry fly in their mouths for several seconds before ejecting it, they are notori-

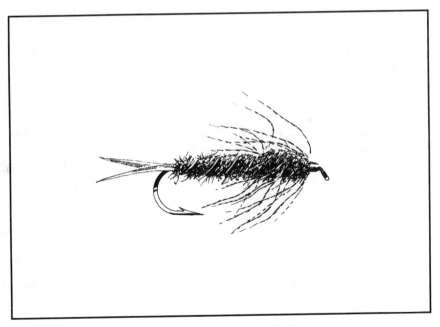

Fig. 32 Simple nymph—tied in the round

ously quick to spit out an artificial nymph. This makes detecting a take on a slack line and striking the fish in time one of the most difficult parts of nymphing.

Nymphs with hard, unyielding bodies flunk the taste test instantly. Those with herl, dubbing, or some other soft material often trick the trout's gums long enough for you to set the hook. And these materials have a further advantage: they tend to play in the current, giving a suggestion of gill-action.

To imitate the nymphal forms of mayflies, I'd want at least the following colors as a minimum selection: yellow, light brown, dark brown, olive, and olive-and-black blended. Sizes #10, #12, and #14 will do, but I'd like to add a yellow in size #16. Two of each size and pattern should see you through any day unless you're an extremely heavy-handed striker.

Caddis Pupae

Good imitations of pupal, or emerging, caddisflies can't be found in many tackle stores. They should have chunky bodies, small, underslung wings, and long, sparse hackles (see Figure 33). A turn or two of a plumage hackle like woodcock or partridge adds appeal. Bodies are almost always dubbed and those of sparkling Antron, which traps tiny air bubbles, can be especially killing.

Soft-hackled wet flies, particularly those with fattish bodies, are more common and, though more impressionistic, will usually fool most trout. Whichever style of pupal imitation you manage to end up with, you should have patterns in light and dark mottled brown, medium dun, green, and olive. Two each in sizes #12 and #14 should start you off nicely.

Stonefly Larvae

Yellow and light-brown mayfly nymphs should imitate most of the common small stonefly nymphs well enough, but you'll need some huge yellows (also blacks, if you're a westerner) for early spring and high-water conditions. These should be at least an inch long and range up to two inches or better. And I'd add the yellow-

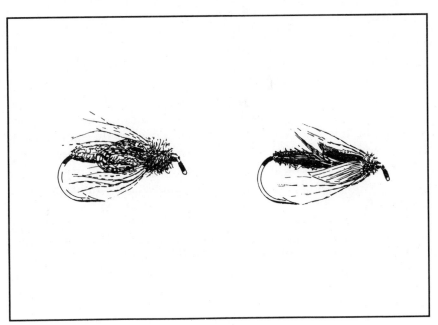

Fig. 33 Caddis Pupae

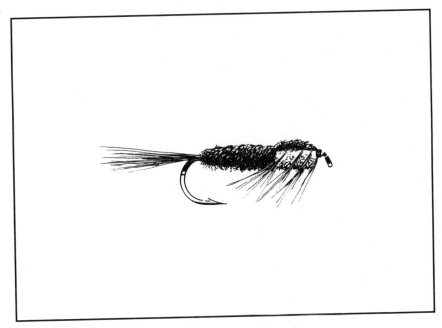

Fig. 34 Montana Nymph

thoraxed, black Montana Nymph in sizes #8 and #6. It seems to have special trout-appeal—East and West—especially on fast streams. (See Figure 34.)

Like mayfly nymphs, stonefly patterns should be tied in the round so that no matter how the artificial rides or turns it always displays the tell-tale belly color. Soft bodies offer the same advantages for sunk stoneflies that they do for other nymphs: longer fish-retention and the illusion of breathing. I'm particularly fond of lemon wood-duck hackle on my large yellows and I think the trout are, too.

Most of your nymphs should be leaded, or, at least, slightly so. After all, a nymph is supposed to get down near the bottom where even the laziest trout may find it tempting. This may make these flies unpleasant to cast—the largest sizes can be brutes—but that's a small price to pay for catching trout on days when nothing else will work.

Streamer Flies

7

S treamers—and/or bucktails—didn't appear until the early part of the present century. They were born in America (in Maine, according to all reports) and quickly became popular lures for large brook trout and landlocked salmon.

With my perfect, 20/20 hindsight, I can't imagine why it took so long to come up with such an obvious fly-style. For centuries, live-bait fishers and trollers had known that large trout (and many other types of gamefish) were piscivorous or "cannibalistic" and that the best bait for them was a minnow—alive or even dead. Yet, until relatively recently, nobody had enough imagination to devise an acceptable fly-rod imitation.

Streamers and bucktails should have absolutely symmetrical wings when viewed from head-on (see Figure 35). If it's the least bit lopsided, the fly will wobble when stripped in—and this, for some reason, subtracts from its fish appeal.

Trout

Streamers are killing trout lures in both still and running water. I've caught brookies and browns as small as six or seven inches long on two-inch streamers, so these lures should not be crossed off as "monsters-only" flies. On streams, I've found them most effective in fast water or when flows are brisk following a heavy rain.

Since most trout streamers run from an inch-and-a-half to three inches long, they're imitating baitfish that are either small, young, or both. Most of these bite-sized minnows are quite translucent—young smelt, especially—so the best representations are

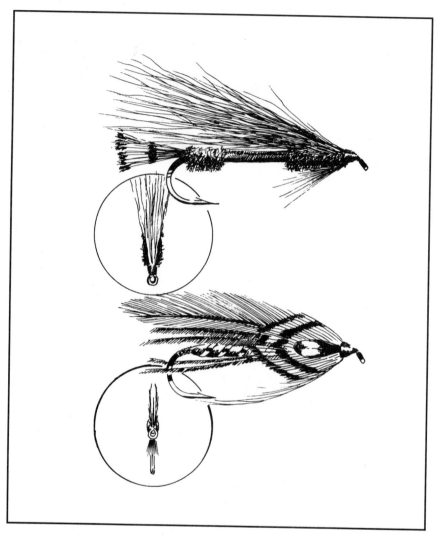

Fig. 35 Streamers, Bucktails—symmetrical wings

sparsely tied out of semi-transparent materials. The chief fault I find with most trout streamers and bucktails is that they're far too bushily dressed. Bucktail is, I feel, both too stiff and opaque a material for the smaller sizes. Hackle feathers are sinuous, let some light pass through, and are justly popular as winging materials. Polar bear is even more translucent, but a bit stiffish. My favorite is white calf-tail, natural or dyed, if taken from tails that are straight-haired, silky, and glassy rather than kinky and chalky. Trout streamers should flex and undulate. The popular marabous certainly do this, but I feel they're a bit too opaque for top trout-appeal.

Patterns

I wouldn't feel the least bit deprived if I were limited to three patterns in three sizes. Trout seem to slash at streamers with a viciousness they rarely display when taking other types of flies and I doubt that a more exact imitation of minnows would move that many more fish.

I'd choose a bright attractor fly like the Mickey Finn to catch the fish's attention in high or colored water. I wouldn't be without a Muddler, or a similar fly, that imitates sculpins or darters. And I'd certainly include an imitation of the most common baitfish coloration like the Grey Ghost. Sizes #6, #8, and #10 on long-shanked hooks will suffice and, since you should be using fairly heavy leaders for this type of fishing, two of each size should see you through any day.

Bass

Streamers and bucktails used for both smallmouth and largemouth bass should be bigger and brighter than trout patterns. Those showing a lot of orange and yellow like the Yellow Perch streamer are usually excellent. An employee of a state Fish and Wildlife department who had the enviable job of estimating bass populations in lakes and ponds by angling stated that, after years of experimentation, an all-orange streamer (with a bit of tinsel) was the most killing lure. Still, I'd like to have a few large marabous in black, white, and yellow because of their tantalizing action. Bass streamers should range from three to four-and-a-half inches in overall length and two in each size should be all you'll need.

Pike

Bass flies are about the right size for chain pickerel, but if you're serious about northern pike you'll want to go even bigger and brighter. Red-and-white or red-and-yellow with generous amounts of tinsel make combinations that are hard to beat. Five to six inches long—or even slightly bigger, if you can cast such a fly—should be about right. And, unless you use an extremely heavy, or wire, leader, carry a good selection. A pike's teeth are nearly as big and sharp as a barracuda's. Extra-long-shank hooks can be very helpful.

Streamers and bucktails are used, occasionally, for other types of freshwater gamefish. Large ones are standard lures for spent, or "black" salmon on Canadian rivers in springtime. However, so few anglers fish for spawned-out Atlantic salmon that I'll just say that mainly bright patterns about four inches long are most popular and leave it at that.

Panfish are quite another matter. Perch, crappie, and bluegills are fond of the fry of their own and other species. Tiny streamers on size #10, #12, and even #14 hooks can outfish wet flies some days. Sparsely dressed patterns—especially bright ones with tinsel bodies—are usually best, I've found, but never rule out the all-black streamer, which they may mistake for catfish fry or young pollywogs.

Salt-water Flies

8

F ly fishing for salt-water gamefish started to gain popularity
thirty to forty years ago and is probably still the fastest-grow-
ing aspect of the sport. Big, strong fish—often large schools of
them—are tempting targets to fly-rodders; and specimens up to
over two hundred pounds have been boated.

Fishing the ocean with fly tackle is not all that new, though.
Dr. James A. Henshall, the eminent bassologist, reported that he
and some friends fly-fished Florida waters successfully for tarpon
(and probably snook and redfish, as well) using salmon flies and
rods back in the 1890s and he laid no claim to being the first to do
so. However, salt water played merry hell with the silkworm gut,
silk lines, and bamboo rods of his day and it wasn't until nylon and
fiberglass were introduced at the end of World War II that ocean-
going fly tackle became durable and reliable.

Briny predators feed on crabs, shrimp, eels, squid, and God
only knows what else, as well as on small fishes, but the basic salt-
water fly is a grown-up, minnow-imitating streamer. These are tied
on strong stainless-steel hooks to prevent rust and corrosion and,
regardless of the overall length of their wings, most are dressed on
regular-length hooks. (See Figure 36.)

Occasionally, you'll find some tied on the rear ends of long-
shanked hooks. This offers the advantage of a length of bare hook-
shank ahead of the fly proper, which is some tippet-protection
against bluefish, barracuda, and other razor-toothed gamefish.

Nearly all schooling baitfish that travel in the upper layers of
the ocean share a similar color pattern. They tend to be white on
the belly, silverish on their sides, and bluish or greenish on top.
This color scheme can be reproduced with feathers, animal hair, or

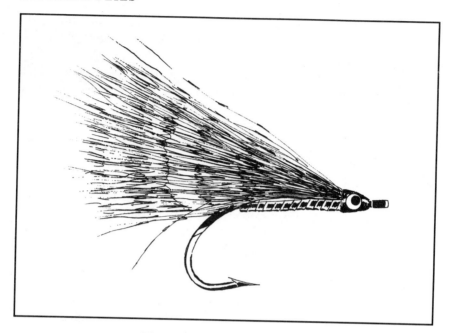

Fig. 36 Salt-water streamer

with new synthetic fibers and a bit of silver tinsel.

Some eye-catching materials have come on the market in recent years—gaudy lurex tinsels, fluorescent yarns, and—a particular favorite of mine—a fine nylon wing-hair that's beaded to catch the light and sparkle. I'm not sure any of these make more accurate imitations, but I'm sure they can be seen at a greater distance and there's a big ocean out there!

When buying or making flies for salt water, be sure they are *durable*—with heads carefully sealed and bodies firmly attached. Both the salt water and salt-water gamefish can wreak havoc on cheap or loose ties.

Though casting a fly that closely duplicates the basic color of minnows may add to your confidence, it may not add much to your catch. All-white flies are popular killers of many types of gamefish. There's a lot of yellow in some of the choicest barracuda flies and many of the top tarpon lures show a lot of red as well as yellow.

The point appears to be that almost any minnow-shaped fly that *behaves* like a small fish in distress will catch fish when they're feeding actively. Why bluefish, surrounded by hundreds of thousands of real, live baitfish, will pounce on the angler's less-likely-looking fly is hard to explain, but it is nearer to the rule than to the exception. Perhaps the lure's obvious *difference* captures the fish's attention and interest. But go ahead and match the "hatch" if it makes you feel more scientific. It certainly can't hurt.

Sparsely-dressed flies may sink a bit faster than bushy ones, but neither sink very well in buoyant salt water. If you really want your fly to travel well below the surface, you'll have to use a sinking line. So a generous amount of wing material is no drawback in the ocean and it just might catch a fish's attention a bit quicker.

As with all streamer flies, wings of salt-water patterns should be centered and symmetrical to insure good swimming action. Hackle, if any, should be on the sparse side, I feel, to help keel the fly. In most other respects, though, salt-water streamers leave little to be picky about.

Recommending sizes and patterns poses a bit of a problem. If you live in the Northeast and fish in the fall for tinker mackerel and snapper blues, you'll need white-winged, silver-bodied streamers about two inches long. On the other hand, if you're going to challenge white marlin or sailfish, you'll want monstrosities eight to twelve inches in length. Most salt-water flies for medium-sized fish like stripers or blues run from four to six inches long and you should start out with a selection of these in the basic minnow colors plus a few yellows and all-whites. If you're making a trip for tarpon, pick up some of the time-tested favorites before you take off. Perhaps the best way to build a good selection is little by little. Buy a few of the local favorites whenever you're out of home territory and pretty soon you'll have a wide enough variety to tempt almost any salt-water gamefish you're likely to encounter.

Flats Flies

Bonefish, the main quarry of tropical, shallow-water fly-rodders, will eat almost anything that moves and quite a few things that don't. As a result, they can be caught, on good days, on almost any small to medium-sized fly of almost any color or shape. However, they do have strong food preferences and it pays to cater to these—especially when casting to sophisticated fish.

While they'll also eat minnows and root out small clams, bonefish, like most gourmets, have a decided weakness for shrimps and crabs. Shrimp seem to be more common on grassy flats while juvenile swimming crabs, the size of a silver dollar or even smaller, seem to predominate on pure sand areas.

Shrimp-imitating flies run from impressionistic to realistic and both seem to work. There are, at present, only a few crab imitations on the market, but you should try to find some and get them in several shades. Swimming crabs tend to take on the coloration of the sand they're traveling over so it's wise to "match the sand."

All flats flies should be tied to ride hook-point up, like the Crazy Charlie series, otherwise you'll snag bottom too often.

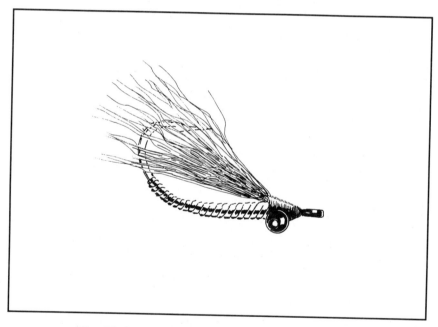

Fig. 37 Crazy Charlie—tied to ride hook point up

They're also less likely to get weed-fouled on grassy bottoms. (See Figure 37.)

Sparse flies will sink faster than heavily dressed ones and this can be a distinct advantage, especially in three- to four-foot depths. However, you can gain much the same effect by using flies with leaded bodies. You should certainly carry some of these—even a few that are quite heavily weighted. Crab and shrimp imitations should be fished on, or very near, the bottom and if they kick up a puff of sand or mud now and then, so much the better.

Most bonefish flies come tied on #2 or #4 hooks, but I'm not sure they have to be that big. If you run across some good patterns tied on #6 or #8 hooks, add them to your collection. They'll make less of a "plop" when you're casting on top of a tailing fish. Don't worry about fish seeing them. Bones have the eyes of an eagle.

Permit are the glamour fish of the flats. They're big, not all that plentiful, and notoriously difficult to tempt with an artificial fly. These overgrown pompano have a strong, almost exclusive, appetite for crabs, so the fly you use for them should look and act like a crab.

The very few imitations I've seen in stores and catalogs are tied out of deer hair clipped into a crablike shape (see Figures 38 and 39). These look realistic enough, but, because of the deer hair, are poor sinkers even when leaded. I'm sure that really good crab flies are yet to come.

I have recently acquired some tied out of over-sized hackles wound on palmer style and clipped top and bottom into the shape of a crab. These are a bit impressionistic, but they sink well and the undulating hackle gives an impression of aliveness that the stiff hair-bodied flies can't match.

Unless you can get a custom tyer to turn out some experimental flies for you, the deer-hair ones are probably your only choice. You'd be under-equipped on the flats without a few in several sizes and shades.

Barracuda prowl the flats looking for schools of "shad," mullet, and, unfortunately, bonefish. When you see one or more cudas nearby, you won't see any bonefish for a while so you might as well make a play for the villains. A big, yellow streamer is

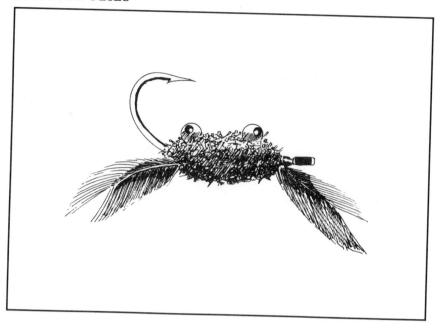

Fig. 38 Deer-Hair Crab

strong medicine—especially if you retrieve it as fast as is humanly possible. Don't expect to land many, though. If they strike at the head of the fly, as they often do, they'll slice through a bonefish leader as if it were made of warm butter.

Sharks, mainly lemons and black-tips, will take flies well and smallish ones often work the flats. Try them with the same fly you'd use on barracuda, but cast as close to their noses as possible because sharks have dismal eyesight. Their abrasive skins may sandpaper your leader clear through, but you should land many of the smaller ones and get at least one great run out of the bigger fish.

You never know what you're going to meet while bonefishing, so it pays to take along your box of regular salt-water streamers while flats-fishing—just in case. Sea trout, ladyfish, redfish, tarpon,

Fig. 39 Clipped Palmer-Hackle Crab with additional top view

snook, and snappers are just a few of the gamefish that inhabit the slightly deeper channels and borders of true flats. They'll all snap up an unwary shrimp or crab, but mainly they're minnow-eaters.

Smallish three-inch minnow-imitating streamers with silver

bodies are about right for sea trout, ladyfish, and the grey snappers that hide out under the mangrove roots. Sometimes you'll find red-fish or mutton snappers up on the flats proper. If you do, try them with a shrimp fly because that's probably what they're looking for up there. In other places, a medium-sized minnow-fly should do the trick. Tarpon and snook like a bigger fly; yellows and reds-and-yellows four to five inches long are the usual medicine for these spectacular fighters.

Improving Your Flies

9

E ven though you have now assembled superior examples of the most useful patterns tied by a skilled professional, you can, believe it or not, make many of them even more effective. This is not to imply that your expert tyer doesn't know his business. But, unless your flies were tied to precise specifications, they will probably conform to the expectations of the mass market—which may not necessarily be the most killing styles and designs. Not surprisingly, it is the most demanding type of fly—the floater—that is most readily altered and improved.

Dry Flies

Trout dries should have their hooks de-barbed before you start fishing with them. This will certainly reduce the damage they'll inflict on released fish, but there are other important—though self-ish—reasons for using barbless dry-fly hooks.

With its barb gone, a hook will penetrate a fish's mouth more easily and more deeply, so you should hook a higher percentage of takes. And, as long as you keep a relatively tight line on the trout during playing, you probably won't lose noticeably more fish. The stub of a barb seems to perform nearly as effectively as the entire thing—which leads me to believe that most barbs are too gross to begin with.

When it comes to unhooking a fish, the de-barbed fly really shines. It will slip out of even the toughest cartilage with a slight tug and the fly won't be mashed, mangled, and covered with slime the way it usually ends up if you've had to wrestle with it. This means that a quick rinse and a few false casts will put it back in good floating condition again. Having to tie on a new fly after each fish can be maddening during a brief hatch.

Then, too, a fly that doesn't have to be manhandled every time it takes a fish will last far longer. Every dry fly's effective life ends when the hackles get mashed flat and no longer spring out perpendicular to the hook shank.

Knocking the barbs off trout hooks is a simple operation. Take a pair of small longnosed pliers, hold them at right angles to the barb, and press down with increasing pressure (see Figure 40). With soft-tempered hooks, the barb will flatten down on the shank, leaving a slight bulge. Hard-tempered hooks will make a slight "click" as all but the root of the barb snaps off.

Hackle-Pruning

Larger dry flies—those on size #12 or bigger hooks—and all variants will cock on the water better and, I feel, appear more realistic

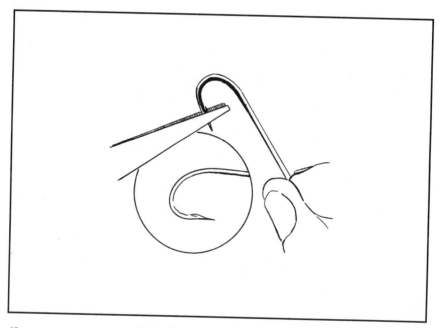

Fig. 40 De-barbing a hook

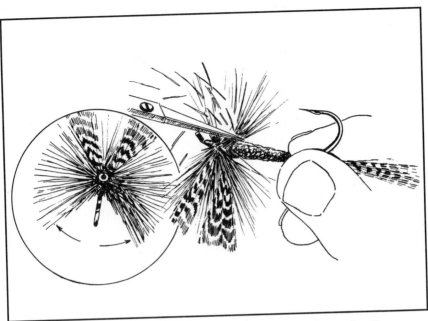

Fig. 41 Cutting the bottom 90 degrees out of a large dry fly

Fig. 42 Untrimmed hackle—an underwater mass

if the bottom 90 degrees of hackle-collar is carefully cut out. (See Figure 41.) This portion of the hackle is expendable since it merely pokes down through the surface-tension and does almost nothing to help float the fly (see Figure 42). This underwater mass has to appear unnatural to the more discerning trout.

Such judicious pruning has further benefits when applied to large variants. They will become 25 percent easier to cast because that much of their wind-resistant hackle has been removed. And it stands to reason that hooking qualities will improve with all that bushy, hook-point-guarding hackle snipped away.

Whether or not this excision is necessary on small flies is a matter of opinion. I have performed this operation on size #18 and #20 dries as a last resort on difficult limestone trout. I think it helped, but I'll admit this may be slicing things too finely.

Splitting Tails

There's one last thing you might do to improve your floaters, but this is winter work. You can split the tails of your flies even though they were tied on as straight as a poker.

Clamp a sample fly in a vise or stick it firmly into a cork. Then, with a needle, separate the tail-fibers into two equal clumps. Press each section sideways firmly until it remains well separated from the other (see Figure 43). Now apply a small drop of clear spar varnish (don't use head-cement—which usually dries a chalky white color) and work it into the fork and base-ends of the tail-fibers. Let this set for three to five hours, then press each clump sideways again until they are separated by at least a 45-degree angle. Give them a day or two to harden up completely and they'll be set for life.

I'd suggest you try this on a fly or two, then test them on the water. If you're as impressed as I am with their superior appearance and stance, you'll set up an assembly line and alter the whole lot.

Although the setae, or tails, of natural mayflies are usually widely splayed, I don't go to all this effort just to make a more realistic imitation. Split tails add more wind resistance as the fly

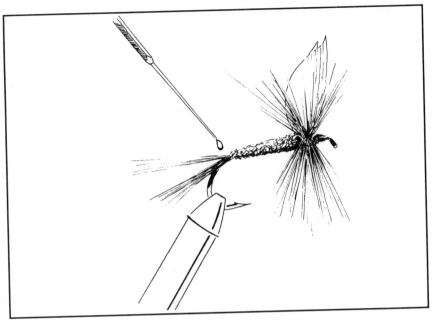

Fig. 43 Splitting tails

flutters down and then grip more surface-tension to help float the heavier end of the hook. They also act like outriggers—cocking the fly with wings straight up virtually every time.

Salmon Flies

Salmon floaters could be de-barbed, also, but I'm not sure there's much to be gained by this. Atlantic salmon are heavy fish and they are usually caught on strong leaders, so penetration is rarely a problem and the customary size #6 or #8 hooks are fairly easy to grip and remove without damage.

I'll admit I'm a devout coward when it comes to Atlantics and leave the barbs on all my salmon-fly hooks. Let's face it: you usually hook so few salmon in a day's fishing that you don't want to risk losing even one.

"V"-Cut

Conventional salmon dries can, however, benefit from having that 90-degree "V" cut out of the bottom of the hackle-collar. They'll cast easier, float just as high, sit wings-up more regularly, and should have slightly better hooking qualities after this minor alteration. Deer-hair-bodied bombers, on the other hand, defy all efforts at improvement. Make your selection at the counter wisely because you'll be stuck with exactly what you bought.

Wet Flies

Trout wet flies can often be improved, but seldom as much as the dries. De-barbing is optional, except for compassionate reasons, because a slimy, mashed wet fly often produces better than a pristine one. If wings or hackle seem too heavily dressed for your taste, you can easily reduce these with a pair of embroidery scissors. Wing fibers or flues should be trimmed from the top and hackle fibers from the front of the fly. Be careful with your snipping, though. Make sure you take equal amounts of material from each side so that the fly will stay in balance and swim on an even keel.

Wet flies with fur, or fur-substitute, bodies can often be made more killing by picking out some of the dubbing. Of course, if they take enough fish, such flies will get shaggy-bodied anyway, sooner or later. But sooner is better, so why not start them out this way? I have a firm belief that the fluttering gills on a natural nymph's body are a strong identifying feature and that they should be imitated as closely as possible.

Salmon wet flies—especially fully dressed, classic patterns—are usually best left alone. It's virtually impossible to prune their complex plumage wings without destroying their color scheme. Hairwing flies are another matter. If you feel that some small, low-water patterns are too heavily dressed, it's easy to thin wings and hackle (evenly, though) down to a sparser appearance.

Nymphs are, by nature, sparse flies, so trimming and pruning are rarely beneficial. However, fur bodies can be picked out with a needle for the same reasons I gave for wet-fly bodies. Look from below at a living nymph in a glass of water. The large, fluttering gills will almost certainly turn you into a dedicated picker-outer.

Streamers can rarely be altered effectively. There's just no practical way to prune whole-hackle-feather wings. Bucktails, on the other hand, like any hairwinged fly, can be thinned, often profitably, to produce a more translucent effect.

Salt Water

Streamers used in salt-water fishing are rarely improved by pruning. The larger baitfish they imitate are rarely translucent and, as I said earlier, a bulky fly just might catch a fish's attention quicker.

If you fish for sharp-toothed species regularly, you can, and should, give your flies added protection. Add a couple of coats of epoxy to the heads of your flies. This is much tougher than any head lacquer and will help prevent premature loss of the fly's wing, hackle, and usefulness.

Flats flies—at least some of the hairwinged ones—will sink faster if thinned out and at least a few of your leaded ones should be quick sinkers. Since it's often hard to identify leaded flies from the lighter ones, it helps to code them. I've solved this problem by putting a dot of black head lacquer on my fastest sinkers, a red dot on my mediums, and a white dot on the unleadeds. This way I can tell at a glance how each fly will perform and the fish don't seem the least distracted by this miniature artwork.

Care of Flies

10

A first-rate collection of working flies is such a valuable asset that it deserves devoted maintenance. Like any other prized material possession, its value and longevity will increase if it receives proper care.

Stowage

When placing your flies in their boxes, there are only two "Thou shalt nots"—but both should be obeyed. Don't try to cram too many dry flies into each compartment. Overcrowding can bend or mash those stiff hackles. And don't consign those fancy, double-hook salmon flies to boxes with flat clips. If you do, the wings will be bent to one side of the shank. The plumage may straighten out again after a bit of fishing, but tying on a double #4 Jock Scott with wings markedly off-kilter certainly won't increase your confidence.

Storage

Winter storage and repair is fairly simple, but certain steps must be taken here, also. It will be comforting to know that, when you finally use a box of flies that have been hibernating, its contents are in tip-top shape and apple-pie order.

Before putting boxes away for the off-season, check each fly individually. Any that appear bedraggled or questionable should be placed in a separate pile.

Repairs

If windings, varnish, or lacquer at the head appear worn, give them a generous coat or two of the appropriate finish and set them aside to dry. Before returning them to their rightful place, make sure the varnish or lacquer hasn't filled in the eye. (Trying to poke your tippet through a varnish-filled eye while fish are rising all around you will stretch even the best vocabulary.) A toothpick is excellent for cleaning a hook's eye.

If the retirement is going to be lengthy, add a sprinkling of moth flakes to the box before you close the lid. Most modern fly boxes are tight-fitting and nearly mothproof, but why take chances?

Reconditioning

Any messed-up, but still sound, flies should be restored to good working condition before storage. This process is identical to the one for rehabilitating freshly used flies described in the following paragraphs.

Make a point of carrying a "used" box with you every time you go fishing. Any small plastic container—perhaps one a shop-keeper has placed your purchased flies in—will do as long as it has a secure lid.

When you want to change to a new pattern or replace a soggy dry with a fresh one, drop it in this box. Don't just stick it in your hatband or that lamb's-wool patch most fishing vests provide. This will almost surely mangle the hackles of a prized dry fly. And any fly is likely to fall out or get brushed off of such a place.

That night, when fishing is over, be sure to take care of these old friends. Remove them from the box and lay them out in a warm, dry place (one with a slight draft is best) to prevent over-night rusting.

Once thoroughly dry, sunk flies are easy to restore. Just fluff out the hackles and stroke the wings back into a semblance of their original positions. Only then, when they look appealing enough to tie on your leader again, should they be returned to their proper place.

Hackle-Freshening

Dry flies, as usual, are more demanding. Many books recommend resuscitating them by holding them with tweezers close to the spout of a steaming tea kettle. The jet of steam will, indeed, restore the fly's appearance, but I'm afraid it will also damage the quality of the hackle.

Fly tyers and materials dealers have known for centuries that dyeing dry-fly hackle-necks in boiling-water solutions reduces even the choicest hackle-necks to mediocrity. Since live steam registers the same 212 degrees F. as boiling water, you don't have to be an M.I.T. graduate to know that you should save the tea kettle for brewing orange pekoe.

A far safer procedure is to place slimy, matted dry flies in a glass of lukewarm soapy water, massage them gently while immersed, then rinse them off under the cold-water tap. Blow on them briskly from the rear until the hackle-collar flares out again, then place them head-down in a good drying location. By morning they should look as good as new and their hackles should be in excellent condition.

Salt Water

All salt-water flies should be rinsed off in fresh water as quickly as possible after use. Granted, their stainless-steel hooks aren't likely to rust. But what about the materials that are lashed onto them? Many tinsels are vulnerable and the lead wire used for weighting bodies can turn into a white powdery substance that can stain body colors after prolonged immersion.

Lastly, check the bottom pockets of your fishing vest every time you quit fishing. If they have been soaked, or even dampened, from deep wading, remove and inspect all fly boxes when you get home. If you find as much as a drop of water inside, open the box and put it in a good overnight drying place. I've seen a box containing over a hundred exquisite fancy salmon flies rusted and ruined because they were put away without this simple inspection.

A Parting Cast

11

I f you have read this far, you understand why I feel so strongly that flies are the most important part of your equipment and that your selection of them can't be too picky. While the very best you can find may, because of the built-in limitations, be none too good, they'll tower head, shoulders, and navel above second-rate ones.

You will probably also have gained a hulking respect for expert fly tyers. Their ingenuity and attention to detail and materials can make—or break—your fishing day. I have never yet met a first-rate fly tyer who wasn't also an avid fly fisher. When you use one of his flies, much of his past experience on the water is handed over to you.

Some of you, having cast a newly jaundiced eye over your current fly collection, may resolve to become serious fly tyers. This is a worthy ambition and one that is sure to make you into a more perceptive and effective angler. But remember: the ability to select the perfect feather for the job and to make it sit precisely the way you want it to doesn't come overnight. It pays to look upon fly-tying excellence as a journey rather than as a destination.

But whether you tie, or buy, your flies, just knowing you have superior ones at your fingertips gives you a huge advantage—over and above their fish-appeal. You will have *faith* in them. Therefore, you will fish them with a concentration and expectation that are, in themselves, half the battle in your continuing struggle to entice and hook the better gamefish.

Bibliography

Twenty-five helpful books that will advance your sensitivity to what makes a superior fly.

BATES, Joseph D., Jr. *Atlantic Salmon Flies and Fishing*
———. *Streamer Flies*
BAY, Ken. *Salt-Water Flies*
CLARKE, Brian, and John Goddard. *The Trout and the Fly*
FLICK, Art. *Art Flick's New Streamside Guide to Naturals and Their Imitations*
JENNINGS, Preston J. *A Book of Trout Flies*
JORGENSEN, Poul. *Salmon Flies*
KOCH, Ed. *Fishing the Midge*
KREH, Lefty, and Mark Sosin. *Fishing the Flats*
KREH, Lefty. *Fly Fishing in Salt Water*
LaFONTAINE, Gary. *Caddisflies*
LEISER, Eric. *Fly-Tying Materials*
LEISER, Eric, and Larry Solomon. *The Caddis and the Angler*
LEONARD, J. Edson. *Flies*
MARINARO, Vincent C. *A Modern Dry-Fly Code*
———. *In the Ring of the Rise*
PROPER, Datus. *What the Trout Said*
SCHWIEBERT, Ernest. *Matching the Hatch*
———. *Nymphs*
SWISHER, Doug, and Carl Richards. *Selective Trout*
SWISHER, Doug, Carl Richards, and Fred Arbona. *Stoneflies*
WALKER, C. F. *Fly-tying as an Art*
WHITLOCK, Dave. *Dave Whitlock's Guide to Aquatic Trout Foods*
———. *L. L. Bean Fly Fishing for Bass Handbook*
WILLIAMS, A. Courtney. *A Dictionary of Trout Flies*